A HORSE'S TALE –
HOW HORSES HELP HUMANS OVERCOME CHALLENGES

BY GENE ARNONE

A Horse's Tale –

How Horses Help Humans Overcome Challenges

Copyright ©2022 by **Gene Arnone**

ISBN Number: 978-1-60571-636-7

Printed in the United States of America

ACKNOWLEDGMENTS

It was my wife Cindy who was the impetus for this book. Knowing my enjoyment and growing passion for the Therapeutic Riding program at Flatlanders, and my thought of writing about my experiences, she gave me three books on horses to start me on my way. As a consequence of this small gesture, along with her ongoing support, this project began. She had to persevere through my constant ideas along with reading various drafts of these stories. Without her help, this book would never have started, let alone finished, for which I am extremely grateful.

Once my thoughts were on paper, my beta reader, Cat Skinner, gave me the honest feedback that I needed to put into words the feelings and emotions to tell the story. This is the third time she has guided me in sharing my experiences on paper, each time helping me grow further as a writer.

Lastly, it was the people and horses at the real Flatlanders who inspired this story and live it every day, for whom I owe all the credit of this story.

IN MEMORIAM

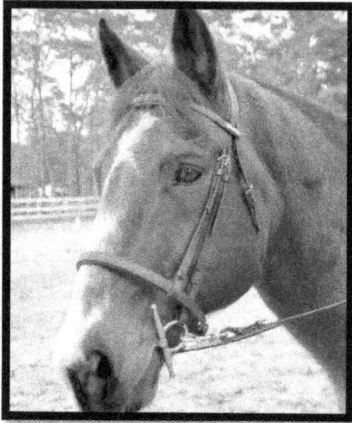

In the final stages of writing this book, Willie suffered a severe case of colic and had to be put down 12 hours later. He was 16 years old, strong, and healthy. He had recently recovered from an injury to his left rear leg and was back in the program to the delight of everyone.

Unfortunately, this is a fact of life in the horse industry and truly a big loss to our program. It is comforting to know that although his life was cut short, his last three years of service brought joy and comfort to those who rode him.

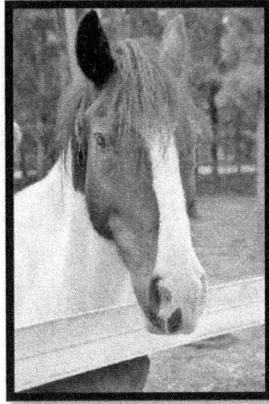

Only a few months later, Chongos, another star of our program, developed an infection and blockage in his abdomen, creating fluid buildup with no significant chance of recovery. We had no choice but to put him down. Chongos was usually the first to catch a visitor's eye because of his gypsy horse appearance, highlighted by the long hair (feathers) which covered his hooves.

When the news of his passing was announced, it was a bitter/sweet time at Flatlanders, impacting everyone who had been involved with him over the last seven years.

Willie and Chongos have been replaced with Prince and Yankee. Flatlanders took ownership of Prince in spite of a disease in his eye which required the removal of his eyeball. Otherwise he is a perfectly trained and well-mannered horse who is going to be a fine addition to our program. Prince came from a loving local family who contributes towards his care and remains invested in his life. He is free leased to us, so now he has a job, where before he was just hanging around with nothing to do. It was a win/win/win for all of us.

An even more fortuitous fate came to Yankee only a few hours from being placed in the kill pen. Yankee used to be in harness racing and, after a less than successful career, became a cart horse for the Amish. As he became older, he was sold to a broker, who was unable to place him and sold him to slaughter. When he wound up in the kill pen, his photo was placed on Facebook and was recognized by his former groom from the track when he was a yearling who purchased him for $500, then donated him to a horse rescue organization. The rescue organization passed him on to Flatlanders.

TABLE OF CONTENTS

Chapter 4

Chapter 5

Chapter 6

INTRODUCTION

Over the last six years since working at Flatlander, I have been frustrated with the general lack of awareness, interest, and value given to Equine Assisted Services. Only added to my frustration, was the growing trend among my peers, of not embracing the concept that "giving back" and "helping others" needed to be part of everyone's daily lives.

My time at Flatlanders Ranch has had such a profound impact on my life that I wanted to put into words my personal experiences and those of others; to not only explain the effect that Therapeutic Riding can have on those with physical and developmental challenges, but also to promote its expansion. Since that first day, the "elevator speech" I have used, (that Flatlanders was a handicapped riding program), did not fully describe its depth and impact; most often just resulting in a "that's really nice" response before moving on to the next topic.

Equine Therapy, Therapeutic Riding, Equine Assisted Riding are all names that have been used to describe the fundamental value of the human - horse relationship. Without the nuances of their technically different definitions, my research, personal experience, and experience of others contained in this book hopefully provides a clearer insight into the value of that relationship. It is my hope that a better understanding of the program will foster its greater acceptance, growth, recruitment, support, and involvement in these types of equine therapy programs in the future.

As an added benefit, it is hoped the "concept of service" can also be rekindled by this story, opening new chapters in people's lives regardless of the beneficiary.

The stories in this book are real, based on my personal observations, although the presentation and characters are fictitious and composites of actual riders and events.

PROLOGUE

Blind Men and the Elephant

by James Baldwin

There were once six blind men who stood by the roadside every day and begged from the people who passed. They had often heard of elephants, but they had never seen one; for, being blind, how could they?

It so happened one morning that an elephant was driven down the road where they stood. When they were told that the great beast was before them, they asked the driver to let him stop so that they might see him.

Of course, they could not see him with their eyes; but they thought that by touching him they could learn just what kind of animal he was.

The first one happened to put his hand on the elephant's side. "Well, well!" he said, "Now I know all about this beast. He is exactly like a wall."

The second felt only of the elephant's tusk. "My brother," he said, "You are mistaken. He is not at all like a wall. He is round and smooth and sharp. He is more like a spear than anything else."

The third happened to take hold of the elephant's trunk. "Both of you are wrong," he said. "Anybody who knows anything can see that this elephant is like a snake."

The fourth reached out his arms and grasped one of the elephant's legs. "Oh, how blind you are!" he said. "It is very plain to me that he is round and tall like a tree."

The fifth was a very tall man, and he chanced to take hold of the elephant's ear. "The blindest man ought to know that this beast is not like any of the things that you name," he said. "He is exactly like a huge fan."

The sixth was very blind indeed, and it was some time before he could find the elephant at all. At last, he seized the animal's tail. "O foolish fellows!" he cried. "You surely have lost your senses. This elephant is not like a wall, or a spear, or a snake, or a tree; neither is he like a fan. But any man with a particle of sense can see that he is exactly like a rope."

Then the elephant moved on, and the six blind men sat by the roadside all day and quarreled about him. Each believed that he knew just how the animal looked; and each called the others hard names because they did not agree with him.

CHAPTER 1

FLATLANDER OPEN HOUSE

My story began in 2015, reading my local weekly newspaper, The Mountain Times. There was an article in Section Three which caught my eye, describing the Equine Therapeutic Riding Program at the Flatlanders Ranch, only five miles from our home in Plymouth, Vermont. The piece described how a small local farm started a therapeutic riding program to serve challenged clients in the Shrewsbury area.

The article went on to say that volunteers were needed to support the program and that a two-hour open house was scheduled for the following weekend. Up until that time all my personal volunteer activities have always involved either my finance background and/or service at a Board level. The opportunity to actually do the work and interact directly with the horses and riders quickly intrigued me and I immediately decided to learn more about the program.

Sunday soon arrived and I found myself surprisingly nervous, but I'm not sure about what. I'd been around horses before, but it had been a while. Dressed in jeans and wearing new work boots, hoping to at least look the part; I was ready to go. As I pulled into the long driveway to the barn, I saw a small group forming, sitting, and standing around a semicircle of hay bales.

Standing in the center was a slim, tall, dark-haired women in her late 50's, whom I later learned was Rachel, the ranch owner. There were about a half dozen other people there, mostly older women and one teenage boy; all of whom introduced themselves to me as I joined the group. Still feeling out of place and lost, I was glad when the program soon began.

"Morning everyone and welcome to our Ranch Open House. My name is Rachel, and I am the Executive Director of The Flatlanders Ranch Program. I and my husband Bob, he's over there by the tractor, bought the Flatlanders Ranch ten years ago."

I learned that Rachel had been riding for her entire life; mostly dressage, which is a rather formal and fancy demonstration of horse and rider skills. Her and Bob traveled around the country the first years of their marriage, while Bob worked in pipeline construction. She was first introduced to equine assisted riding in Ohio 15 years ago, which soon grew into her "calling," as she became a certified instructor there.

After twenty years of semi-nomadic life, Rachel and Bob decided that they wanted to settle down in one place. After a year of searching, Bob found a supervisor opening for an excavation company here in southern Vermont, and they bought the Cooper property and turned it into the Flatlanders' Ranch and the chance for Rachel to open her own equine assisted riding program.

After that standard introduction, Rachel continued in a noticeably different tone: "For me, this program gives me satisfaction like I never have experienced before. It provides me with the opportunity to change lives every day. I have seen tears and emotion when horse and rider exceed everyone's wildest expectations. One child said his first word while riding a horse, one rider who had a stroke is able to work on balance to be able to ride a horse, another child with very low self-esteem is now confident in their riding skills which has made them more confident in situations outside the barn. The stories go on and never get old. There is a lot of work and frustration that is involved in running a program like this, and there are times when I wonder why I'm doing it, but it's those other moments that make it all worthwhile."

Pretty heavy stuff for the first five minutes of an orientation, but something was quickly drawing me in. Maybe this was my opportunity for the more direct hands-on contact that I had been missing from all my previous service activities.

Now it was time for a tour of the property. We first went into the barn where all the stalls were empty, and the building was quiet. Never really having spent any time in a barn, my first impression was how organized and neat the entire area was. The stalls were clean with sawdust spread over what looked like a rubber mat and each had a window to the outside. The roof was 20 feet high with lighting and fans for ventilation. I saw that each of the stalls had a horse's name on it: Chongos, Buddie, Willie, and Garfield.

All the horses were out in the pasture, as I learned they spend their entire day outside, using these stalls only during lessons. During harsh weather they moved into the lean-to in the pasture, otherwise they preferred to just graze outside the entire day.

7

At the end of the barn there was a door that opened into the tack room where all the saddles, bridles, and reins were organized for each individual horse. Every horse had two saddles; English and Western, which were used based on individual rider needs.

As we walked out of the barn to the lesson area, Rachel gave some background on the program: "The Flatlanders Ranch is a certified member of PATH Intl. founded in 1969 as the North American Riding for the Handicapped Association (NARHA) to promote safe and effective therapeutic horseback riding throughout the United States and Canada. Today, PATH Intl. (Professional Association of Therapeutic Horsemanship) has 873 centers in countries all over the world supporting 70,000 riders with special needs through a variety of equine-assisted activities and therapy programs. The Flatlanders' program currently serves 75 riders in central Vermont, providing 1,000 individual lessons each season."

"There is often inconsistency when referring to PATH programs, some calling it Equine Therapy, Equine Assisted Riding, Therapeutic Riding among other names. PATH defines their overarching Program (EAAT) Equine Assisted Activities and Therapies. Activities are provided by a Certified Therapeutic Instructor which can be expanded to Equine Therapy involving a Licensed Clinical Social Worker specifically trained for equine activities. The Flatlanders Ranch currently is limited to Therapeutic Riding activities, also called Equine Assisted Riding."

Here I thought that this was just a small riding stable doing good in our community. I didn't realize that there was even this level of need in our area, let alone the program being a part of such a large organization.

Rachel continued: "The Flatlanders Ranch opened 10 years ago with a focus on therapeutic horseback riding as a form of physical and mental therapy. All of the instructors are PATH certified and have since developed a full spectrum of equine-related activities such as Horses for Heroes for veterans and first responders, Yoga on Horseback, Silver Saddles for Seniors and a Barn Rats program for young riders."

"The riders served at Flatlanders may have paralysis, multiple sclerosis, autism, Down syndrome, substance abuse, traumatic brain injury and other co-morbidities. The focus of the Flatlanders' program is to increase strength and flexibility, improve motor skills, promote speech and cognitive reasoning, and help build relationships and social skills."

As we were introduced to the program horses, the duties of the volunteers were described and I quickly realized that our role was 'down and dirty', covering a spectrum of both riding and support activities. As a volunteer, our responsibilities included grooming and saddling, leading and side walking during lessons, along with feeding and pasture turnout. It was made clear however, that volunteers would only be asked to do activities that they were comfortable with, and we could be involved as much or as little as we wanted.

With that as background, the next two hours quickly immersed us into the two basics of the program: horses and riding.

HORSES 101

As we left the barn, we continued the orientation passing the gazebo where visitors sat to watch during lessons. As our small group approached, one of the horses, young, completely black and stately, started to immediately walk towards us, and put his head over the fence to greet us.

"This is Imus, my horse," Rachel introduced the unofficial greeter for all Flatlander visitors. "Although Imus is only two years old and in training for the program, he is a perfect example of the horse – human connection."

We then proceeded to learn how the fascinating horse - human relationship has led to the benefit of both. Man's first encounter with horses was for the basic need for food. It didn't take long for man to realize that the horse was also valuable in providing transportation and power for work. Over time, recreation followed, and it was at this stage that a more personal relationship developed. Unlike other animals, horses have many qualities similar to man which gives them a unique opportunity to form a mutually beneficial and deep physical and emotional connection.

I guess Imus got the memo, as he nuzzled up to anyone who wanted to stroke him.

"Just put you hand out palm side down and let him smell you." Rachel demonstrated. "If you put it the other way, he will think that you're offering him a treat. Also, you can give him a gentle stroke on the side of his head; he likes that."

Of course, we all had to try.

We also learned to never stand directly in front or behind a horse. Horses have eyes on the side of their head, which gives the ability to see almost 180 degrees on each side. But because of that they have a small blind spot directly in front and back. Like humans, they always want to keep people close to them, in sight.

"You may actually not realize it," Rachel explained, "But horses are prey and flight animals and value the safety of the herd. They thrive in groups and suffer from loneliness just like humans. Socialization plays a large part of their lives and can have a significant psychological impact on their behavior."

As we stood talking, the other horses started to slowly walk over to the fence to see who was there and what was going on. In spite of their size, there was a friendly and curious energy that I felt as they approached. In a matter of seconds, it felt like it was a reunion of old friends. At first, I was a bit intimated by these 1,000 pound animals, yet quickly relaxed seeing their friendly welcome.

The family and social orientation of humans is mirrored in a horse's relationship with the herd and forms the potential for an emotional connection. Man is an emotional creature, and the sensitivity of horses as prey animals allows them to be aware and adjust to those feelings, the energy of the horse often times overpowering humans. It has been shown how the natural calm of the horse can influence those around them. Not only do horses recognize emotions, but they can remember and respond to them in their behavior.

Rachel further explained, "Horses communicate with humans through sounds, behavior and energy. Snorting and whinnying are the words horses use to communicate, along with behavior, especially with their heads and ears; all giving clear messages. Energy is by far a horse's greatest and most subtle form of communication. Although it may require many years of experience for humans to fully understand, it forms the basis for our program."

We then learned that aside from the relationship value, it has been shown that horses can provide physical and emotional benefits from the therapy riding experience. Balance, flexibility, strength, and confidence are all outcomes of equine assisted riding. On the emotional side, riders experience patience, bonding, verbal, and nonverbal communication, which combined, can provide life altering benefits. It is this history and the similarity of natures that make the synergy of man and horse a benefit to both, and this forms the basis for Therapeutic Riding.

The training of a Therapy Horse isn't simple, and because of the rider complexities and needs, the criteria is rigorous. Often like humans, having the right personality is not something that can be trained; deep inside the horse either has it or doesn't. There is not a specific breed that is preferred over another, although the temperament of stallions quickly eliminates them from consideration. Geldings (castrated male) and mares, possessing certain critical traits, all have the potential to be therapy horses. Also, the body types of different breeds lend themselves to the various physical needs of riders, resulting in a program that requires horses which cover a full spectrum.

There are two main criteria which define a true therapy horse, in addition to general physical wellbeing and good behavior when grooming, tacking, bathing, and loading:

1. Docility level 1 or 2 (laid back, calm) on a scale of 10 (high intensity, racehorse) - The temperament of a therapy horse is critical to their success in meeting the needs of their riders. Riders with intellectual, developmental, and physical challenges all require patience and tolerance from the horse in their lessons so they can relax, balance, and focus. This characteristic is especiallly important when mounting and dismounting, when the rider is most active and at risk. Also, during lessons, riders are also prone to improper balance and movements, which would agitate most horses (for example, riders with cerebral palsy).

2. Desensitivity to actions, noise, and activities in close proximity - the lesson plan for riding contains various unique activities vs normal riding. Rider may be asked to lay down backwards or forwards to the horse to increase their balance and flexibility. Activities will include the throwing of balls and rings which may bounce off the horse's body while the rider constantly moves about. Also, for the safety of the rider, in addition to the horse leader, there will be one or two side walkers, stationed directly

alongside the horse, giving the horse a sense of confinement. Lastly, the sounds of music or chimes are also integrated into the program, only adding to the chaos from the perspective of the horse, who must maintain calm.

Overall, the demands placed on a therapy horse, over and above that of a normal trail horse, call for a very unique and special animal for an optimal horse - human relationship to flourish.

RIDING 101

Rachel brought out Chongos for some hands-on training for our various responsibilities. It started with leading a horse, which I had never done. The operative word is "leading," in that you lead and walk along side of their head/shoulders, and the horse will follow. You never look at the horse while walking, just look and walk in the direction you want to go, and the horse will follow. It was amazing how easy it was, although Rachel warned me that horses would test their riders, especially those who were newbie volunteers.

Taking the lead line from me, Rachel went on, "Although you will not be instructing, it is important that you know some basic techniques so you can improve the rider experience. It begins with the horse approaching the mounting block. You want to make sure that the horse is very close to the ramp so that the rider is not trying to mount over an open space. As the rider is getting on, first make sure that the stirrups are down, and you are always ready to react should the rider lose balance when getting on the horse. Don't rush anything, let the rider and instructor set the pace of mounting."

As I led the horse toward the mounting block, I realized this part was a little more difficult than it looked, since the opening to the mounting block was only 24 inches wide and the horse needed to stop right in the middle, making sure he didn't move. The horses were trained to stand even when challenged with a sometimes agitated rider. After a few tries and thanks to the horse cooperating, I was able to accomplish the task.

It was then that Bob joined us. He introduced himself with a deep voice, initially striking me as being a typical "ranch hand"; tall, muscular, with a three-day beard.

"You're just in time to join us," said Rachel, "I need a rider so I can demonstrate the volunteer's role in a lesson." Rachel then proceeded to use poor Bob as an example of the various methods which are used to mount the rider on the horse, given their different limitations.

This part was really eye opening. I had never thought about helping someone with cerebral palsy get on a horse or assisting someone with the left side of their body immobile from a stroke, or even just the general fear that a 5-year-old with autism might have next to such a large animal.

"Every rider is different," Rachel said, "and it is important that we make this initial part of the ride as effortless as possible; it is the key to success or failure. A bad experience at the onset could delay or even end a rider's participation in our program."

Although I still did not appreciate the full benefit of the program, this comment demonstrated to me the importance of small actions to these often fragile and challenged riders.

While my head was still processing this last lesson, Rachel never missed a beat, "Next we leave the mounting block and bring the horse and rider into the arena."

As I lead the horse out of the mounting block, now with Bob in the saddle, Rachel added, "Your job is just to ensure that the rider maintains their balance. This is a good time to greet and give some encouragement to relax the rider."

After entering the arena, the leader is supposed to stop the horse and the instructor will check the girth (saddle strap around the belly) and adjust the stirrups before beginning the lesson. As a new volunteer, I would primarily be a side walker, the person who stood on either side of the horse for safety and support.

After taking lead line from me and positioning me at the horse's side, Rachel went on to the next part of my lesson, "Your primary role as a side walker is to provide physical support through one of three positions depending on the skill level of the rider."

For the least stable rider I held the saddle with my forearm over the thigh of the rider to provide maximum support. As the rider progresses, I moved to an ankle hold, and ultimately just walked and watched to the rear of the saddle. I listened to the instructor who gave commands to both me and the rider. During the warmup stage of the lesson, this could involve me helping the rider to reach or turn during their exercises.

I quickly felt comfortable with each of these positions as we walked around the arena. I didn't realize it until we began walking, but the ground is very soft dirt, almost the consistency of walking in the sand on the beach. This is to protect the horses from injury as they perform their activities. I soon learned that a typical lesson day could involve nearly 3 - 4 miles of beach walking!

As we walked around the perimeter of the 80' by 160' arena, Rachel explained that "The next part of the lesson will focus on the goal the instructor has set. It could be starting and stopping the horse, controlling right, left, and back commands, trotting positions of two point, sit trot and posting at the walk and trot."

My role was only for physical and emotional support. As the lesson came to an end, there is a cool down phase, primarily for the rider to relax. Often, they would take their feet out of the stirrups to help, with me again providing support as necessary.

As we left the arena it was finally time for the dismount, which Rachel said was done from the mounting block or as rider advanced, directly to the ground. She emphasized that "the instructor will have full responsibility for this, with you only involved to the extent the instructor requires it."

This role I was about to step into was extremely important to the success of the program and provided much to the experience. We were told that as we develop a relationship with the riders over time, we will find this more gratifying and rewarding than we could ever imagine.

As my training came to an end, the two hours had blown by and everything seemed simple enough until driving home when I stopped and thought about all the steps involved in a routine ride, not to mention dealing with the complexity associated with each rider. I would soon learn first-hand how all these important pieces came together.

CHAPTER 2

THE CHALLENGES OF THE RIDERS –
MY PERSONAL EXPERIENCES

We take physical health for granted until that life changing event occurs, and everything turns upside down. It could be at birth or the result of accidents or conflicts, but regardless, the accommodation and rehabilitation of the body has limits and sometimes feels impossible. The mental aspect can be even more frustrating and difficult, often times with limited potential for a normal life.

The Flatlanders Therapeutic Riding Program addresses both these challenges and as a volunteer I saw, firsthand, the improvement possible. Parents would be brought to tears when their child accomplished something as simple as steering a horse around a set of cones or remembering a series of commands and executing them flawlessly. They would say things like, "I never thought that my child would ever be capable of that."

Recently we had a rider's parent call to thank everyone at Flatlanders for providing such a wonderful experience for her son. She said it was the first time he just got to be Robby and not the child with disabilities.

There is one memorable day that sticks out most in my mind when Harry said his first word, "Whoa," after 17 years of silence! It brought everyone to tears, and even though it was a onetime event, and probably not consciously done, it had a tremendous impact on us all.

Therapeutic Riding involves riding lessons for individuals with disabilities with the goal of teaching horsemanship while using the natural therapeutic benefits of the horse. Combined, it contributes positively to their cognitive, physical, emotional, and social well-being.

The lesson is taught by a riding instructor with a special certification in safety standards and adaptations to teach a rider with disabilities – so it's often also called adaptive riding. The instructor is not a therapist providing therapy or the goal of rehabilitation, but rather is an equestrian instructor for children and adults with disabilities. The focus of these lessons is skill development and progression. Depending on the disability, benefits of horseback riding include improved coordination, relaxation of spasticity, increased muscle tone, self-confidence through enhanced self- image and improved learning, concentration, and spatial awareness.

The stories that follow will not only document the successes of the Flatlanders Program, but hopefully encourage others with physical and mental challenges to improve their lives by joining programs around the world such as ours.

JACOB

As I look back over the last six years, there is one rider who stands out from the others: Jacob. While his name may not be at the tip of everyone's tongue, the mention of his name immediately brings a smile to their face. He is a hard rider to work with, and sometimes you wonder just how much progress you are making, as you repeat the same instructions every week. But seeing the joy in his face and the pride and confidence he has about riding, albeit often misplaced, still demonstrates the impact our program can have on individual lives. One of the main benefits of equine therapy programs is the many opportunities to practice communication and language, by giving basic directions to the horse and feeling a sense of accomplishment when the horse follows those directions. My first and now regular experience with Jacob follows a fairly standard script.

The silence and calm of the day is suddenly broken from afar with a loud call out, "Hi mister Gene" as Jacob arrives.

As always, I'm greeted with a BIG hug and the same question, "Can I ride Ben today?"

I respond with the same answer, "Ben is not in the program and is owned by someone else. You're going to ride Garfield like every week."

This twenty-five-year-old has an energy level that can quickly drain you if you're not prepared and is a challenge to keep focused. It is my job to manage his activities and improve social, communication, and behavioral skills. Improvements are small and often quickly pass, but over time there have been some.

Our initial checklist every week includes making sure that his boots are on the right feet, that his fly zipper is closed, and that the carrots he always brings for the horses are left on the bench until after the lesson. While doing this I'm peppered with information ("I just came from Dunkin Donuts") and questions ("Do you like Dunkin Donuts?") often times Jacob doesn't even take a breath between subjects.

As the horse leader when Margaret, his volunteer, brings Garfield out, Jacob immediately throws his arms around his neck giving him a BIG hug and kiss, followed by the comment, "I thought I was going to ride Buddie today."

As we mount and go into the ring, there is always a request to be made, usually about having his brother (who lives in California) or his girlfriend ride with him next time because they would really enjoy it. Next week it might be someone else. He's just a very caring person.

As the lesson begins with a warmup lap around the arena, Jacob proceeds to call out hello to all the horses he sees out in the pasture. I say, "Focus Jacob, focus" to no avail, which becomes the mantra of the entire lesson. Although fully capable when he puts his mind to it, he struggles with both remembering and executing the commands, which leads to moments of both celebration and frustration.

When the lesson is over, Margaret takes him over to the horse's stalls, where he distributes with great focus the carrots, he always brings into each of their food buckets. He then says goodbye and asks Margret if she'll be there next time and suggests that maybe he can ride Ben at the next lesson as he heads off to his ride home.

MICHAEL – DD RIDER

Of all challenges faced by the Flatlanders riders, I've had the most experience with the Developmentally Disabled. My time here has created an entirely new appreciation of their lives. My close hands-on contact as Mr. Gene gives me a brief moment to walk a mile in their shoes, seeing their challenges firsthand and watching how they cope with the outside world. I've also learned how quickly they develop a relationship with the horse, not only benefitting them physically and emotionally, but at the same time giving me a clearer insight into their thoughts and behavior.

"Helping people to live the lives they choose" has been the cornerstone of the Arc of Windsor County for over 25 years and The Flatlanders Ranch is a proud partner in making that a reality. Our therapeutic riding not only benefits riders physically, but more importantly, develops self-confidence and independence.

Our relationship with Special Olympics also allows our riders to experience inclusion and community, through competitive athletics, where every single person is accepted and welcomed, regardless of ability.

The unique relationship that these riders develop with their horses leads to the interpersonal relationships required as they make their way through life. Riders quickly sense the unconditional love and support from their horse, which in turn opens them to the social interactions they will need in their own independent lives. Self-confidence is also gained as they progress in their riding abilities, opening their future to enhanced opportunities for how they might live.

When I told Michael that I was writing this book and needed his permission to tell his story, he emphatically said "Ok," so I pulled out my phone and he started to talk about himself and Flatlanders, which resulted in a very surprising perspective of him and the impact of our program.

"Hello - my name is Michael; I am 18 years old and have Down Syndrome. When people ask me what Down Syndrome is, I tell them it's an extra chromosome. A doctor would tell you the extra chromosome causes an intellectual disability that makes it harder for me to learn things. Some of my classes are in a 'resource room,' where kids with many kinds of learning disabilities are taught at a different pace."

"When my mom first told me I had Down Syndrome, I worried that people might think I wasn't as smart as they were, or that I talked or looked different. I can't hide my special needs because of the distinctive facial appearance most of us with Down Syndrome share. I just want to be like everyone else, so sometimes I wish I could give back the extra chromosome. But having Down Syndrome is what makes me, me. And I'm proud of who I am. I'm a hard worker, a good person, and I care about my friends."

"It's true that I don't learn some things as fast as other people. But that won't stop me from trying. I just know that if I work really hard and be myself, I can do almost anything. I can't change that I have Down Syndrome, but one thing I would change is how people think of me. I'd tell them, 'Judge me as a whole person, not just the person you see. Treat me with respect, and accept me for who I am. Most importantly, just be my friend.'"

Michael has been riding at Flatlanders now for five years and is getting to be a pretty good rider. This year we suggested to his parents that he enter the State competition to be held in Rutland. There were two classes that he entered, Equestrian and Trail. Mary has been working with him all season to help him learn the course and skills that he needed to participate.

"Last Saturday Mom and Dad drove me to Rutland and Rachel brought Buddie from the ranch. Everyone keeps telling me to relax and that I'll do just fine, but still, I couldn't sleep last night. This is my opportunity to show all the kids at school that I can win awards and trophies just like them. I know that I'm not as smart as them, and can't play the same sports as them, but I can ride a horse."

When Michael arrived and saw 100 other riders, he was a little overwhelmed. Some of them wore fancy riding clothes and had beautiful horses, and he was just wearing jeans and my Flatlanders' sweatshirt.

As he just stood there taking it all in, Mary called him, "Hurry up Michael, we're up in fifteen minutes. we're going on the obstacle course first."

Ted, his volunteer, was also waiting to take him around the course, and to try and get him calmed down. Ted had a big smile on his face and said, "You got this Michael" as he led him into the ring.

29

The judge with a clipboard stood at the starting line and announced, "Michael Johnson number 23," and turned to Michael and said, "You can go whenever you're ready."

Ted said, "Just focus."

Michael took a deep breath and said, "Walk on Buddie." and off they went.

"Funny I don't remember much about the ride," Michael said afterward. "I remember turning and hearing myself saying the commands to trot, whoa and back, just like I do in my lessons at the ranch and then, it was over. People were clapping and I heard Ted say, 'You did it!' When we left the ring Dad had a big grin and it looked like Mom was crying. Rachel came over and said, 'Good job, take a little rest before the riding demonstration.' Some of the other riders and parents came up to me and congratulated me."

Soon it was time for the next event and Ted lead Michael into the ring again. In this event, there were five other riders in a big circle walking around the ring, with the judges in the middle. The announcer called out each of the rider's names as they entered the ring and told them to keep walking and follow her commands. During this event each rider had to demonstrate whoa, go back, then walk on and change direction. She then had them stop and trot down the side. After all that was done, they lined up in the middle of the ring and waited for the judges to compare their scores.

Michael recalled, "I had a big smile on my face because I knew that I did everything right. The announcer was saying we were all winners as the judges gave out Green, Orange,

Yellow, Red, Purple, and White ribbons; I got the Green one, my favorite color. As soon as I got off Buddie I gave him a big hug and thanked him. He tossed his head and gave out a snort. Ted came over and pinned the ribbon to my sweatshirt."

"Quick Michael, we have to go back over to the obstacle ring for the awards ceremony there." Ted said, as he led Buddie alongside.

Again, the announcer called each of the rider's names as they walked in and lined up in the middle. Michael was excited again, "This time I got the yellow one. I couldn't believe that I had won two ribbons!"

"Mom said that I fell asleep in the car on the way home holding my ribbons with a big smile on my face. I was tired that night and hung my ribbons around the posts of my bed. I could hardly wait to tell the kids in school on Monday."

31

Stacy – Physically Challenged

Flatlanders Ranch is proud to be selected by Central Vermont Medical Center (CVMC) to participate in developing equine assisted programs for stroke rehabilitation in Vermont. Our program is based on the human - horse partnership and focuses on the key aspects of recovery: speech, cognition, and physical fitness.

Stroke is a leading cause of death in the United States and is a major cause of serious disability for adults. Much has been written about prevention and treatment, but we are only beginning to explore the full potential of recovery alternatives to shorten the return to a more normal life.

People who have experienced a stroke may experience challenges resulting from the area of the brain affected by the stroke, such as the loss of the use of a limb, difficulty finding or understanding words, or balance problems.

Flatlanders developed a program to work with these challenges to assist those who have had a stroke to regain strength and balance through the physical activity of riding horses. It is the energy and unique horse to human connection that makes this all possible

Stacy is a 45-year-old adult who was drawn to horses at a young age. While in the Brownies she was introduced to horses in summer camp and immediately wanted to get involved. Her parents signed her up for lessons at a local barn and soon she was riding two or three times a week. A couple years later they even leased a horse part-time so that she could ride more often. When she reached high school however, academic, and extracurricular activities ended her riding career. Fast forward 15 years, she was now established in a marketing career and rising up through the corporate ranks and living in the Burlington suburban area and had the ability to buy a horse and ride again. She had been riding on a regular basis again for almost 10 years, with her horse, Baron a central part of her life.

And then it happened. It was supposed to be a routine appendectomy, but something went wrong with the anesthesia, and she suffered a stroke and was in a coma for 5 days. When she awoke, the entire left side of her body was paralyzed, and her speech slurred. Her memory and thought process was also affected, the extent of which only time would tell. Over the next 6 months she was gradually able to regain some movement but riding and her corporate career were over; doomed to a life of long-term disability.

One day, during one of her physical therapy visits, a new therapist who learned about her case suggested equine - assisted therapy. Stacy knew nothing about the program at the Flatlanders Ranch but joined what would soon be a life-changing experience.

I was there the day Stacy's recovery journey began. She found herself at The Flatlanders Ranch about to ride a horse for the first time in three years, or at least that was the plan.

After hearing Stacy's story and seeing her for the first time, I wasn't sure how she would ride, let alone benefit from the program. When she arrived on crutches there was a look of determination on her face. Debbie, her instructor, started with an introduction to the program and how it can strengthen muscles and help in maintaining balance.

"We're going to do this in three steps today," Debbie said, taking me over to a barrel laying on its side. "First we're going to sit on this and stretch a bit."

Since Stacy had limited use of her left side from the stroke and couldn't place her full weight on her left foot, she was not able to mount the normal way by lifting her right leg over the saddle.

"So first we are going to learn how to mount from the right side of the horse," Debbie continued. Stacy had never mounted that way, yet she felt immediately comfortable, and balance was not a problem, since both feet still remained on the ground.

After about five minutes of stretching Debbie said, "OK now let's get off and go meet Suzy."

"Suzy? Who's Suzy?" Stacy asked.

"She's our wooden riding horse, right over here. We use it as part of our Barn Rats program," said Debbie with a smile, as she took Stacy over to a five-foot-high wooden horse with a small step next to it. "Now we're going to climb on just like we did with the barrel, but this time it's into a regular western saddle and your feet will be off the ground."

Having always ridden English, I'm sure the western saddle looked like an overstuffed recliner. After taking a deep breathe, Stacy slowly lifted her left leg over, with our help, and sat in the saddle. This was a significant accomplishment since this time she had to focus on balancing, and once on, had no connection to the ground. Debbie and I were there to help steady her and soon was comfortable and able to shift her weight while maintaining balance.

"I think we're ready to get on a real horse," Debbie said. "If you are, Chongos is waiting."

As we walked over to the mounting block and climbed the three steps to the top, we could see Stacy's apprehension grow. Although Chongos was smaller than Stacy's horse Baron, Stacy said "He looks so big. It's been two years since I've been this close an animal this size. I'm not sure that I can do this."

"Just relax, Mr. Gene will be our leader and he has total control of Chongos," said Debbie. "Margaret will be your side walker on the right side, and I'll be on this side, if you need any help. You'll just be going along for the ride, just like on the barrel and Suzy."

As I brought Chongos into the mounting block, Stacy just stood there, trying to calm herself taking one deep breath after another and saying, "I can do this."

Then, just like the two times before, she lifted her left leg over the saddle, Margaret guided her foot and helped position it on the other side as Stacy sat down in the saddle. Chongos shifted his weight a little as she got on, but Stacy held her balance just fine.

"Let's just sit here a minute until you're settled," said Debbie. "See, that wasn't so hard."

"Good job!" chimed in Sally.

"I'm on a horse, I'm on a horse again," Stacy said with joy, followed by a cry of "Let's do it!"

"Walk on Mr. Gene," Debbie said with an ear-to-ear grin and Stacy's ride began. Although tentative at first, we slowly walked around the arena. With each step I could see Stacy relax and feel more confident, and as we completed the first lap, a smile slowly crept across her face and a tear rolled down her cheek. There was no doubt in my mind that Chongos had a lot to do with that happening.

Our first ride was no more than 15 minutes, just a few laps around the arena, with the some starts and stops and steering around barrels. But it was a lifetime accomplishment for Stacy.

When it was over Stacy said, "I know that I will never ride like I did before, but today has given me a new outlook on life both physically and mentally and the hope that Baron and I will be riding together again soon."

ALBERT

The mission at Rutland Special Services is very similar to the Flatlanders in that we both help our clients overcome challenges they face every day. The only difference between the two programs is that we use horses. A child on the spectrum can easily feel left out or excluded from social situations most of us take for granted. A therapy horse is a supportive and gentle friend that who they can depend on as they follow the direction of the therapist.

A critical component of our program is the empathy and communication which horses have with humans. Riders are taught to communicate and care for the horse. Our horses are trained not to respond to riders if they act differently or make loud noises and sudden, abrupt movements. Horses also give riders on the spectrum a chance to experience the role of a caregiver and develop emotional connection. This bond can help improve social and communication skills with family members and therapists.

Autism is described within a mental spectrum of behaviors. It is my opinion we are all somewhere on that scale and that society has drawn lines which define the parameters of normal. I have seen that clearly demonstrated in the behavior of individuals, some of whom serve as both challenged riders and competent volunteers, within our program at Flatlanders. We all have our problems and challenges, and our riders clearly are on the further ends of "the spectrum" but my experience has taught me that it is only a matter of degree which separates me from some of the riders.

When I first met Albert's father, he described his son in these terms: "He's a very smart and independent person; and very stubborn. He never shy's away from telling you exactly what he thinks, and it's always so logical. But there are times when simple things confuse him and he is naive about a lot of things in the world, taking things at face value and thinking that everyone is truthful all the time. We especially have to watch him when he goes on Amazon. He has OCD (Obsessive Compulsive Disorder) and social anxiety. Autistic people's minds work differently than ours, and once you realize and accept it, he is most loving and open son any parent would be proud of."

When I told Albert that I was writing book about Flatlanders and I wanted to write about him, Albert said that he wanted to tell his story himself. This is his first-time public speaking, so I turned on my phone and the following is a transcript of what he had to say.

"My name is Albert, not Al. I am sixteen years old, and I am on the spectrum. People tell me that I am high functioning which I guess means that I'm smart. I'm not sure, I'm just me."

"I go to the Special Services School for kids like me. I used to go to regular school but there is too much noise, and they make fun of me. I can't play any of their games and don't understand what they are talking about. I like going to the Special Services School and will graduate next year."

"I like to be left alone so I can do the things I want, like build, read and watch National Geographic. I never forget anything. Sometimes people interrupt what I'm thinking and tell me to do things; I don't like that."

"I have been riding since I was seven, and now at 16 have grown into a strong and independent rider. Today, like most days, when I show up for lessons my first responsibility is to help get Garfield ready for our ride. Since he already has an earlier lesson, the main change I need to make is placing a bit in his mouth. Midge has taught me how to do it, sliding the metal piece into his mouth. A horse has front and back teeth with a space in between where I slide the bit after opening his mouth with my thumb from the side. Sometimes I have trouble and Midge, or Margaret offer to help, but then I eventually do it."

"I then bring the horse out to Margaret to hold as I mount him from the block, and we enter the arena. I'm one of the best riders in the program and our lesson normally goes very smoothly."

"When we're finished, I tie him up in the outside stall, unsaddle him and put it away in the tack room. Now I get to thank Garfield for a nice ride by giving him a nice brushing, which he thoroughly enjoys. This is our time together and everyone leaves us alone and allows me to talk with him about whatever is bothering me. He understands me better than anyone. My father usually says, 'come on Albert, we have to get going', so I say my goodbye and walk him back into his stall."

41

"I know Cate, Jacob, and Luke from Special Services, and even though we are all autistic, we are not the same; that's why they call it a spectrum. We all love riding and without the program here at Flatlanders, our lives would be very different."

LUKE

Luke is a 19-year-old rider on the spectrum who quietly and very politely arrives with a simple, "Hello Mister Gene."

He will never look at me directly but always has a series of questions which can run a gamut of topics in no particular order and varies each week.

"Mister Gene, do you know about computers?" he asked one day. "Yes, I do" I said, feeling technologically savvy for my age.

"What clock speed do you run? I'm building my computer and don't know if should use 2.0 MHz or 3.0 MHZ?"

Quickly regaining my composure, I asked, "Which were you thinking?"

To which he replied, "3.0."

"Well, I think that would be good," I said and then quickly change the subject.

"Mister Gene, do you think this will be a bad year for cicadas? I'm not sure if it's every 13 or 17 years that it will be bad."

Or the day he asked me where I lived, and I told him on Salt Ash Road in Plymouth. Luke lives about 10 miles away from me yet he immediately said, "That's right near Osprey Lane."

"Do you know someone from there?" I asked.

"No," he said. "I was just reading the tax maps from there the other day, with my father who is a realtor."

But surprisingly once he mounts Changos all the talking stops and a flat look comes over his face as he goes off into another world. Like other lessons, we first stretch and practice the basic commands of walk on, whoa, back and in and out weaving through the cones; all perfectly executed in total silence with the exception of the commands he gives the horse. As the lesson progresses the instructor asks him to follow more detailed and lengthy commands, again all done perfectly.

When our lesson is done, he again says, "Thank you Mister Gene," gives his horse a hug and walks to his father waiting in the car. I'll never forget one evening when he had a late lesson, and it was growing dark. He stopped about halfway to his car and just stood there for about a minute looking up at the full moon on the horizon, and I couldn't help but wonder what was going through his mind.

The instructors receive reports from his Special Ed teacher periodically, which mentions disruptive behavior and not understanding and following directions, yet the rider I know does none of that, which convinces me that equine therapy clearly makes a big difference in his life.

KEN – ON THE ROAD BACK

The Flatlanders Horses for Heroes program is the one that Rachel is most proud of. It incorporates equine ground and riding with life skills necessary for our returning veterans to adjust both physically and mentally to life back home. The program is designed especially for those suffering from Post-Traumatic Stress Disorder (PTSD) and Traumatic Brain Injuries (TBI).

In designing the program to deal with these challenges, we focus not only on strength, balance, and flexibility but also impulse control, stress tolerance and emotional awareness, using the horse as a biofeedback machine for both the instructor and rider.

Our service personnel have fought to preserve our freedom, and for many like these riders, at a very dear cost. We must be certain that if our wounded service personnel and veterans need and want this kind of help, that they will get the best PATH International has to offer here at the Flatlanders Ranch.

Over the last twenty years, war for Americans has been far away, and many of us do not connect with either the why or need for our involvement. The all-volunteer army further separates our direct involvement other than reading and hearing few minutes about it on TV. Another change is that current warfare results in more of our young men returning home are physically or emotionally wounded than killed. It takes a special person to volunteer and fight these wars, and we are proud here at The Flatlanders Ranch to have a program to help them transition back to life at home.

The calm, peaceful environment of southern Vermont, the smell of fresh hay and friendly horses are in sharp contrast to the chaos of a war zone or the bustle of the VA Medical Center. Here local veterans can participate in a non-traditional therapy program called Horses for Heroes to help them transition.

Horses for Heroes is a program for both veterans and first responders. The program uses both mounted and ground equine assisted activities to assist in physical and emotional healing. Our horses are highly sensitive and mimic human emotions. Working with horses in a therapeutic setting offers instant and constant feedback to participants, requires physical strength and balance, and is highly motivational; which when combined provide the perfect rehabilitation opportunity.

Working with veterans often involves a unique set of skills for an instructor, the most crucial of all is the art of listening either directly to the rider, or equally important, the feedback that the horse provides. We can never know or understand their experiences, but through the Horses for Heroes program, we can see the rider's emotions and reactions and provide activities to help them deal with them. Of all the difficulties our riders face, our heroes often prove to be the most challenging, but in turn, also provide the most rewards.

I was in the Air Force during the Vietnam war and because of that, today I receive discounts on my taxes and many purchases, and often hear "thank you for your service" when people realize that I am a veteran. In fact, I joined ROTC in college to finish my degree and was stationed in Upper Heyford, England for my entire four years in the service, hardly very dangerous or heroic.

At Flanders the wounded veterans in our program are true heroes with physical and/or emotional wounds received during their service to our country. It is inspiring to hear their stories, although they are often times reluctant to share them, except to fellow comrades. Being a small part of their "road back to normal" is extremely rewarding to me and the other members of the staff and is our way to show gratitude for what they have sacrificed.

I clearly remember the first time I met Ken. I knew that he was a wounded veteran and tried to establish some contract with him saying that I was in the Air Force during the Vietnam conflict forty years ago, however, never saw action. I knew his experience was very different than mine and asked him if he was willing to share his story. Surprisingly he said he was very happy to talk about it and that was a recommended part of his therapy.

"I was about halfway through my first tour of duty in Afghanistan. I had just come back from mail call and was happy to receive a letter from home; it had been a while. Me being away had put a lot of pressure on my wife Cathy, trying to raise two young kids, one with special needs, but we both knew that when I volunteered to be deployed."

I stood outside in the chow line of the food tent with a hint of a smile on my face, thinking about my family back home and the feeling all of us soon being together again. The sun was shining, and the temperature was 100 degrees, I don't care what they say about dry heat; it was hot! Bob was in front of me and Bill behind, both somewhere else in their own thoughts too.

The next thing that I remember is waking up in the hospital in Germany some two weeks later, with my head heavily bandaged and throbbing. The nurse came over came over and grabbed my hand saying, "Ken, it's good to have you back, how are you feeling?"

"Where am I? What happened?" I said, as things slowly came back into focus.

"Just relax, you're in the hospital in Wiesbaden, and you're going to be all right. The doctors will come in soon and explain everything to you."

What I was able to find out later was that there was a surprise mortar attack on the camp, one of the shells apparently landing only 10 yards away from where I was standing. Bob and Bill never made it home, I was the lucky one. All my body parts are here and functioning, it's my head that hasn't fully recovered and probably never will. I'm fortunate not to have any memory of the attack and haven't experienced any PTSD like some of the other veterans I met during rehab.

After about two months at the Army Hospital in Albany New York, I was able to return home to my family in Plymouth. Albany being only 2 hours from Plymouth gave my family the opportunity to visit me and get acclimated to the new me. It was at the Flatlanders Ranch that the Army was using equine therapy in a new approach to rehabilitation. Initially it focused on my regaining balance and strength. My headaches were under control, but my stability was shaky. Ed, one of the instructors, had recently completed a PATH program geared to Veterans and I was his first student.

The first lesson was a rocky one. All morning I laid in bed with one of my headaches. You never know when they're coming or how long they'll last. The medication works but I'm usually groggy the rest of the day. I was excited to start the program and didn't want to miss that first day, so when I arrived at 4:30 pm I wasn't totally myself. Ed, a veteran himself from Vietnam, and I just talked for the first half hour. We compared our experiences, as he gradually became a fellow comrade who could understand and relate to my issues. I later learned that this bonding was a key component to the program.

In the service I was in great shape, 6-foot 1 inch and 195 lbs. but that was now changing quickly. I was gaining weight from the inactivity and medication, now approaching 220 lbs. so Willie was the clear choice to handle me. Ed also put me in a western saddle making it easier for me to balance. That first ride, or should I say walk, around the arena was so relaxing. It felt like sitting in the overstuffed recliner. I just closed my eyes and forgot, for that moment, all that has happened.

To my surprise, riding came naturally to me, and I progressed quickly. After only a few lessons, I was trotting and in full control of the horse. My frustration however came from not only missing lessons because of headaches and medication changes, but from mental lapses that came in remembering a sequence of commands or even forgetting simple things like where to hold the reins. Ed is very patient with me and keeps repeating, "Ken, this is a long process to recovery and you're going to stumble along the way. Stop seeing only the current failure but be proud of how far you've come."

"I'm also fortunate to have another veteran rider with me each week. He name is Warren and he served around the same time as I did, but in Iraq. He was riding in a truck down the road and ran over an IED (Improvised Explosive Device). He was fortunate not to have any serious physical injuries but has been suffering from Post-Traumatic Stress Syndrome (PTSD) since his return. His description of what his life is like and the demons he faces often makes me feel fortunate. He feels that he is constantly on guard and that something is always right behind him. Then all of a sudden certain places, things or sounds trigger him right back in that moment, and he experiences it again with all five senses. He says it's like being afraid of the monster under the bed."

"He also is an independent rider, and we enjoy riding together. I think Garfield and Willie have formed a relationship with us, somehow sensing our needs and providing the unconscious support we need. We have both experienced a conversation with our horse, even though no words are spoken."

"Having the opportunity to spend time with Warren before and after lessons has also been a great benefit to both of us, not having to explain how we feel or what we are going through. Unlike other veteran activities, our time together here, both on and off the horse, allows us the opportunity to forget the challenges we face and just become our old selves again. Thanks to The Horses for Heroes program our life today goes back and forth between two worlds, and thanks to riding, increasingly back to one of a normal life."

"It's been almost two years now and thanks to the VA, I'm getting back to normal. I still get flash backs and go back into that depressing time, but for the most part, I'm fine, although my memory gets confused sometimes and my medication gets out of whack. Physically, everything works, but I realize that things will never be the same."

CHAPTER 3

WHO ARE THE HORSES?
IF THEY COULD TALK

When I first started volunteering, I began working regularly with a horse named Cortez. I had been his leader for a few weeks when, one day, I went out to catch him for lessons. As I entered the pasture, he looked up and immediately started to walk over towards me. It had been an especially frustrating week for me, nothing seemed to be going right. As I hooked up his halter to lead him out, I was startled to hear him start speaking to me, "Hey Mr. Gene, take a deep breath, everything is fine. Your problems are nothing compared to the riders you'll help today. Just relax, enjoy and be thankful,"

As we walked to the arena, I actually had a conversation out loud with him and felt like a totally different person by the time lessons started. This was the start of a regular communication that we would have during the season. Cortez passed away that winter, but he taught me to be open to a horse's empathy and energy and the impact it can have.

Over time I have seen and learned that just about everyone in the program has real or subconscious interactions with our horses. This is not unlike man's relationships with other animals, yet different maybe because of their size. I especially see it in our riders, and the immediate bonding that takes place.

53

It is during these interactions that the personalities and moods of each horse reveals itself, no different than in people.

In the wild, horses roam in herds. There is always an alpha who rules the roost, finds food and safety. There are the betas who are the horses in the middle who argue among themselves for a pecking order and sometimes challenge the alpha for the head position. And then there is the omega who is the last in line and usually very happy in that position finding peace and quiet.

The Flatlanders herd changes each time a new horse is added to the group. And change continues to occur over time.

Garfield is the alpha in spite of his laid-back appearance.

Willie, who has been with Garfield for years and always stays close, has similar traits but not as strong a personality thus falling into the Beta position.

Buddie also falls into the beta position, and wears his mood on his sleeve, especially on days that he feels lazy and doesn't want to work.

Chongos is the omega and veteran of the herd, having been at Flatlanders for the last seven years. He just goes with the flow, although sometimes he can get a bit temperamental. He tends to get pushed around by the other horses but stands up for himself when necessary. He does that sometimes with his program leaders too.

As volunteers, we see the horses go through various stages of behavior during the course of the season. We are told that these changes are all natural and not unlike what we humans go through during our lives. My first reaction was that we were working the horses too much and that they needed some time off. Then I learned that Flatlanders limits its horses to no more than 11/2 - 2 hours a day, 5 days a week, or about 15 lessons per week. This should give them ample time to rest but does not necessarily result in what appears to be a happy, energetic horse. It is important that instructors monitor three behaviors: Tired, Bored, and Burnt-out. The instructors will then change how they use the horses accordingly.

Given our lesson schedule, if one of our horses starts acting lazy or stubborn it usually means that they are bored, typically because they are always in the same area, doing the same drills, at the same speed. This is why we try to change the lesson routine with trail rides and sensory trail activities. Often the instructors will take the horses out on a training ride, changing pace and exercises to make things interesting. I was surprised watching these rides and had a hard time recognizing the same horse I'd just used in a lesson which I thought needed a rest.

Tired is unfortunately something important to avoid but inadvertently happens because of weather and scheduling, causing extra workload on the horses for a short period of time. Instructors are very sensitive to this and use ground lessons and the other horses to minimize that from occurring.

Lastly there is burnt out, which must be avoided at all costs. Burnt out means that the horse is physically (tired) and mentally (bored), overworked, and has experienced too much of the same thing for too long. To ensure that this does not occur, Flatlanders attempts to always have one extra horse in the herd so that everyone in the herd has time off. The long-term health of the horses is always their primary concern and will not be compromised.

Regardless of their standing in the herd, personality or mood, the horses demonstrate an understanding and tolerance when they are with the riders and a clear connection to their individual needs. This is something that I can feel with each one of them as a leader/side walker, just as I did with Cortez. The talks that I had with him, back and forth to the pasture, I now enjoy with each of them.

I could go on telling you more about each of them, but I'd rather you hear it straight from the horse's mouth.

BUDDIE – DRAFT HORSE

Us horses are the key to making this program work, so don't be surprised that we have a lot to say. I am an 11-year-old chestnut draft horse.

Being a draft horse, I'm also the biggest of our group at 16 hands and 1,200 pounds. In spite of my size and strength, I have great patience and a calm temperament, perfect for the larger riders in the Flatlanders program.

Before coming here, I worked on a farm in Maine where people came to experience what life was like in the 1800's. They would live in an old farmhouse with no electricity, milk the cows, make butter and grow their food. That's where I came in. My job was to pull the plow and wagons that the guests used in their daily activities. The work wasn't that hard, since the farm was small. The hard part was being driven by people, both young and old, who never worked with a horse before and were given only five minutes of lessons how to do it.

They were constantly steering me in different directions and pulling on my bit, often resulting in a tug of war. The farm shut down four years ago and Rachel and Bob brought me to their ranch. I didn't realize it then, but that farm work prepared me for some of the same behavior that I experience here at Flatlanders. Yet it's different here. The riders I work with now are trying hard to deal with all kinds of issues and I feel a need to help them however I can. They often apologize for hurting me and I tell them, "That's ok, I know you didn't mean it."

There is a lot of activity and traffic around the ranch every day, most of which doesn't bother us. Though there is one thing which always catches our attention, and that's a horse trailer. When one pulls into the barn area, we all immediately stop and try to get as close as we can to see what's happening, because it always means someone is coming or going, neither of which is good.

There was some commotion around the barn last week and we noticed that Alabama was not put out to pasture after breakfast. Alabama is a 15-year-old thoroughbred from the next pasture, and belongs to Miss Amy, one of the ranch's boarders. The vet arrived earlier and then a trailer. It seems that Alabama has come down with colic which is a very serious and often times deadly condition for horses.

Most people don't realize that our intestine is the major digestive organ in our body and is 50 to 70 feet in length. It lies in the main body cavity and is constantly shifting around. Colic takes the form of a blockage in the intestine either

58

caused by a buildup of material or a twist in the intestine itself. It's like constipation in you humans. While only 15 - 20% of horses will get colic in their lifetime, it is 50% fatal. Other horses have told me that it is extremely painful and if the blockage remains in place too long, the blood supply is stopped and the intestine dies, which could untimely lead to our death. Medications, internal and external massage, and surgery are used to address the problem. Unfortunately, even when successful, the likelihood of recurrence is high.

A while ago we saw Alabama get into the trailer and drive off and he hasn't come back. They also took his name off the stall. All this had a special impact on Sam, a blind horse in his pasture. Alabama was the shadow always nearby to help guide Sam around, often with a nudge to him or other horses who got in his way. Supporting, helping, and protecting Sam has been Alabama's role since he got here.

Now Sam is lost and standing alone in the back corner of the pasture. I'm not sure what will happen next?

Yesterday another trailer pulled up to the barn. We all watched closely as a different horse was led out and put into a separate pasture by himself, but it wasn't Alabama. Today we found out it was Hobo who was being held in quarantine for 21 days and would be taking Alabama's place in the next pasture.

Equine Rescue

When faced with the loss of a horse, the Flatlanders quickly turns to local horse rescue programs. Although not discussed in this book, equine rescue programs throughout the nation serve as a second chance home and transition for hundreds of horses annually. Their sole mission is to provide a loving sanctuary to abandoned, neglected, abused and slaughter-bound horses. These not-for-profit organizations buy horses at auction who would otherwise be sold to kill brokers, people who buy horses to sell them for meat to people in Mexico and Canada. About 90% of the animals that go through these slaughter lots are in perfect health and are a source of horses to programs such as ours.

If you have ever had the opportunity to work with any type of animal which has been rescued, you can clearly sense the acknowledgment and appreciation they demonstrate for being given that second chance. Although it can't be proven, I believe that the temperament and understanding they display toward our riders is their way of saying thank you.

GARFIELD

Hello, my name is Garfield, and I was born in 2011. I came from Ohio with my friend Willie last year and we both have the WHF brand on our hips from our previous owner. We were both rescue horses and came from a program that retrains horses like us to perform certain tasks. I didn't know what therapeutic riding was, but I've really enjoyed my new life.

I am a Haflinger, which is a type of small draft horse, and I am leader of our herd. With that comes both rewards and responsibilities. I am responsible for the group's safety and am alert for any situation which threatens the herd's well-being. Sometimes the other horses don't listen to me, especially Chongos, who likes to think of himself as more of a free spirit, but overall, the four of us make a great team. As leader I get to eat and drink first whenever I want and can control where we graze and wander during the day. I am a chestnut with a golden mane and tail and am relatively smaller than the other horses at 14.3 hands (59 inches to the shoulder).

People say I walk different from other horses and have a distinctive gait that humans describe as energetic but smooth. I guess that's good because a lot of the newer riders like to start on me.

My muscles make me look strong, yet I am very graceful when I canter. Haflingers were developed for use in mountainous terrain, and we are known for our stamina. During World War II, breeders liked horses like us that were shorter and more draft-like, and we were favored by the military for use as packhorses. Haflingers have many uses, including light draft, harness work, and various disciplines such as endurance riding, dressage, equestrian vaulting, and therapeutic riding.

Trail rides are the most fun I think for both me and the rider, especially Michael and Clint. Our ranch is right next to Calvin Coolidge Homestead in Plymouth, and we ride the trails through the little village where in the late 1800's and early 1900's our 30th President lived, died, and is buried. The trails take us through woods and farmland, often spotting deer grazing. Trail rides for me are sometimes a little scary since my nature is always to be on the lookout for predators and I don't have my herd to protect me. I keep alert most of the time, but the deer blend in, and like me, are always on the lookout; so, we often scare each at the same time. That's why there is always a horse leader attached to me, so I don't hurt the rider.

Not long ago I was taking little Cate for a ride. After a few laps around the arena doing our warmup exercises, Midge asked Cate if she wanted to go on the Sensory Trail and was met with a smile and big "Yes."

The Sensory trail is the biggest test for a therapeutic horse because by definition it goes against horse fears. We are grazing animals who like peace, calm, and safety and the sensory trail challenges it all. We walk over bridges, through a space between trees where pieces of foam tickles my belly, up and over another bridge called the 'see saw,' then stop by a tree to play catch, on to another with chimes, and finally back out over the bridge. There is peace, calm and safety challenges all the way especially as balls bounce off my head and chimes ring in my ear.

It took me a long time in training to get comfortable with all of this and Willie still won't do it. Those Quarter Horses sometimes get a little too uppity for their own good.

Cate must have had fun because I heard her talking, laughing, and screeching the whole time. When we got back, I sensed a special happiness energy from everyone, which felt different from other lessons. As Margaret, (the volunteer leader) put me back in the stall, she gave me a hug and said, "Good job Garfield, you made Cate very happy today."

While most riders speak their commands to me, some of my riders communicate with me mostly through their minds and bodies. Slight pressure on my side or rein and I immediately know what they want to do. Sometimes I can just sense where they want to go or do, like our bodies and minds are one. I heard the instructor say that I was a great biofeedback machine, whatever that is, for her to get a better sense of the riders' feelings.

I often think that I have the best of all worlds. Not only do I have the human connection everyday, but I get to do what I love to do and that's run, or as you humans call it, trot and canter. I get to do it in the pasture whenever I want and in the arena during lessons. One of my lessons is with two independent riders, Ken, and Warren, who do not require leaders or side walkers and who are more advanced in their riding skills, although still with challenges.

There is something different when Ken and Warren are in the ring and Buddie joins us too. I don't fully understand but Buddie has a theory. Most of our other riders have physical or emotional challenges which they have to deal with every day and which they are learning to overcome. Ken and Warren, on the other hand, seem to be dealing with the frustration of trying to regain something they had before, but may never have again. For them it seems to be a struggle between trying to be who they were, versus accepting and dealing with who they are now.

CHONGOS – GYPSY HORSE

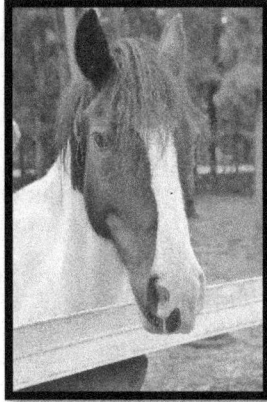

I know horses can't talk, but we do have an amazing ability to communicate and show emotion and that is how I typically like to express myself. My real name is Yaven's Longo Chongos. Not sure where that came from, but at the Flatlanders they just call me Chongos. Humans describe me as a Gypsy Vanner and I love to pull things and be ridden. I got my name from pulling the Gypsy's caraVAN. I'm an easy going guy who loves children because of their friendliness and openness. Some adults try to control me; if they only knew how I much I want to please them, maybe they would act different.

I was born in 2009, but don't remember much of my time before coming to Flatlanders five years ago. I know I was rescued though; it a feeling that all rescue animals have and something we are all grateful for and will never forget. I like to describe myself as a rescue horse here to rescue riders.

I'm 14.3 hands tall, that's 59 inches from the ground to my withers (shoulder blades) and I weigh 1,000 lbs. To humans that means I am midsize, but broad and strong. I am black and white, with a long mane. At Flatlanders, I usually get either children, smaller adults, or difficult to manage riders - again, no problem. I have a job to do, and I love doing it. I love to reach around with my neck and give young riders a 'gypsy hug.'

The one thing I am sensitive about is when people treat me like I don't have a brain. Yes, it is only 1/3 the size of you humans, but I'm a very quick learner with great empathy. I am very serious about my business and have a saying - don't confuse a workhorse with a working horse!

All the riders always want to go on a trail ride rather than their normal lesson. I can feel how peaceful and relaxed they immediately become, normally in total silence, except for Jacob, who is talking all the time. They look out for deer, although it's my hearing and eyesight that normally finds them first and I hear, "Chongos, why did you stop? What do you see?"

It's then that the instructor says, "Look at Chongos' ears moving in all directions; he's trying find what may be hiding around us."

Because I am a prey animal dependent on grazing, my hearing and eyesight is more highly developed than humans. My ears are cupped to better capture sound and my eyes are large and located on the side of my head, which gives me the ability to see almost 360 degrees. However, because of the location of my eyes, two different parts of my brain are independently used in my sight comprehension. That means if I am walking straight in one direction and turn around, what I have been watching now becomes an entirely new experience. Also, I'm blind directly in the front and directly behind me and that's why I tend to keep moving my head to get a full perspective of what is around me, always on guard.

Although we look laid back and content, we horses do get bored, especially when we have a three-lesson day in the arena. Today was one of those days. It was hot and the flies were having a feast on me. My white body and feathers (long hair around my lower leg and hoofs) attracts more flies to me than Garfield, Willie, or Buddie. I guess that's a small price to pay for my added beauty. When I am out in the pasture, I have a fly mask they put over my head and a sheet to cover my body. It works, but I'm quite a sight to behold. I've gotten over the embarrassment and jokes from the other horses.

To help keep the flies away, before my lessons the volunteers spray me with repellent, but it never works. I'm constantly shaking and biting to keep them away. The worst are the horse flies; four times larger than regular flies with a bite that shoots through my entire body. The side walkers are always telling the riders not to get upset when I move like that, but I can't help it. It's hard for the leader too, as they and I are constantly tugging back and forth with each other. That's when I like to have one of the more experienced leaders like Amy, who knows what's happening and keeps the lead line loose for me to scratch.

WILLIE – QUARTER HORSE X

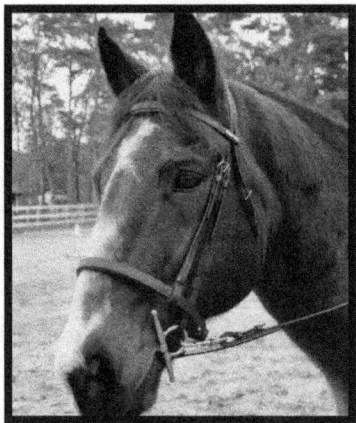

Me and my best bud Garfield have been at The Flatlanders ranch since last year. I'm what humans call a Quarter Horse Appendix or X. I'm 16 years old and stand 15 hands, chestnut in color with a white star on my forehead. When I first heard the X, I thought there was something wrong with me, but another Quarter Horse X in Ohio explained to me that it just means that we're not pure bred. Quarter horses are an American breed of horse that excels at sprinting short distances. Our name is derived from our ability to outrun other horse breeds in races of a quarter mile or less; some of us have been clocked at speeds up to 55 mph. My hind legs are strong and allow me to change direction quickly, making me especially valuable for ranching activities.

So how did I end up here in a therapeutic riding program? Well, that's because of the X. It seems some of my family got hooked up with other breeds and these mixed relationships gave me some other characteristics, especially an easy-going personality which makes me perfect for the Flatlanders Program. The fact that I am also a gelding, like all the other horses in the program, doesn't hurt either.

Because of my size and quarter horse breed, I love to be in the arena. Many of my riders are independent which means physically and emotionally they have progressed to riding without the need for horse leaders and side walkers. They have also advanced to trotting. and one rider even to cantering. That's where the quarter horse in me shines and I can be the real me. Because of their independence, often we have two riders in the same lesson, and we practice doing various exercises together. This is where I met Ken and Warren; I can sense their determination and sense of pride when they rode, especially when they synchronize their riding.

People ride by the ranch on a regular basis and stop to look over the fence. Garfield and I like to walk down to greet them and hear them say how pretty we are and what a wonderful and relaxing life we have. Well let me tell you; the life of a therapy horse is not all grain and grass.

This is what a typical day for me looks like:

The morning light wakes me up, (yes, I sleep standing up most of the time), and soon Rachel or one of her helpers, brings me in to the barn for my morning grain. Each of us has a different meal, I know that because one day they gave me Buddies' breakfast. I don't know how he can eat that stuff, but he's happy.

Anyway, then it's then back out to the pasture to graze on what little grass grows in southern Vermont, and some hay. I hear Rachel sometimes joke about us saying that all horses do all day is eat and poop. Well to a certain degree that's true but I chalk that up to just plain healthy eating and a well-functioning digestive tract. On an average day, at 1,000 pounds, I will eat about 15 pounds of grass and hay and drink about 7 gallons of water. Add that to 50+ feet of intestines and we leave quite a trail of waste behind (no pun intended) requiring 9 - 10 poops a day.

This is where another friend of mine, Amy, comes to visit me every day. she brings the hay and scoops the poop. We've become quite good friends and as part of her pay, we get to go on trail rides together. Amy used to put out open bales of hay and we would have a feast. But lately she puts it in barrels that have small openings, which takes us longer to pull out and eat. When she saw the look on my face the first day, she said that I was eating too much, and this was a way to slow me down.

Then the real day begins, with the first volunteer or rider coming out to 'catch me' for a lesson. Most of the other horses are resigned to the fact of work every day and just stand or even walk up to them to be taken for lessons. But I'm not like that. Sometimes I don't feel like working or I don't know or like the person, so I just walk away. Eventually I give up and accept reality, but sometimes that takes a while and might require a second person to catch me.

After being groomed and saddled, (the love and attention vastly differs depending on who's doing it), the lesson begins with very different experiences awaiting me each time. It's really nice when my rider and I have bonded, and we know

71

how to work together. Other times there is not a connection, and we seem to be going in different directions both physically and mentally. Most importantly, there are my special riders whose feelings and emotions give me the feedback that I enjoy the most. Physically, I get a little beat up sometimes, but I understand that they are not doing it on purpose, so I don't mind, and that hug and kiss I get at the end makes it all worthwhile.

The day comes to a close after 3 or 4 lessons. I'm back in the barn for evening grain and then out to pasture for the night. This is the quietest time of the day where, just us horses have a chance to swap stories and find a space for the night. I'm told that I normally sleep about 5 hours a night standing up, I don't know, horses can't tell time and don't have watches anyway. I like to lay down for about an hour during the night knowing the other horses have my back.

Heat and cold, snow and flies, old and new people make each of these days different. Buddie, Chongos and Garfield's lives are all about the same and we do this for most of the year. There are times during the season when we get a horse vacation, days without lessons or with long periods of rest. While those days are relaxing, I miss my time with humans and the unique relationship we enjoy together; never forgetting the ongoing gratitude I have for being rescued.

So that's what it's like to be me. Overall, not a bad life to have.

CHAPTER 4

THE INSTRUCTORS – PURPOSE AND PASSION

So many people today recognize that there is more to life than just living. They feel that we each have a purpose or calling for which we are placed on this earth. This feeling seems to be strongest in two periods of our life, both entering and leaving our mid-life. In between, we seem to get caught up in making a living and raising a family.

There are some in every generation who have found their purpose and follow their dreams wherever they may take them, regardless of the financial rewards. We see them throughout our community every day; they are our teachers, firemen, EMTs and clergy. Others don't start their journey until later in life, piggy backing from their previous employment, or starting second chapters in totally different directions.

During my time at Flatlanders, I saw that sense of purpose on a regular basis, especially in our instructors. They are clear demonstrations of individuals whose calling is now using their passion of riding to help those with physical and mental challenges.

Throughout my six years of volunteering, I've had the opportunity to see into the lives of these instructors. It is my hope that sharing their stories will open the minds and hearts

73

of others looking for direction in their lives and will inspire them to use their knowledge and skills to help those less fortunate.

MIDGE – SENIOR INSTRUCTOR

When I first met Midge, she told me that her husband had passed away the year before and that she had just moved in with her daughter and grandkids. They had lived in Springfield Massachusetts until her husband retired after 40 years as an accountant with Baxter Travenol and moved to Woodstock Vermont ten years ago to be closer to their grandchildren. It was then that she learned about Flatlanders and found her passion as a certified instructor.

She tells her lifelong story of riding in very real terms:

Riding has been my life for over 50 years. Being a good horse person isn't a job, but a passion. I was lucky that my parents helped me buy a horse; Crocket was $1200. I paid for half and worked for his care and my share of his board. I had to get up before school, ride my bike a mile to the barn, feed and turnout my horse, ride back, shower (sometimes!) and then hurry so I didn't miss the school bus.

I didn't do after school sports because I had a horse to take care of. Most weekends I babysat both Friday and Saturday nights to make enough money to pay my half of the board.

Growing up in rural Massachusetts, there were no fancy horse shows. The first Sunday afternoon of the month during summer we had riding competition at the State Fair Grounds, as part of the local 4H program. On those days I had to get to the barn really early to feed and get my horse ready and pack our things. Then I quickly returned home, showered, and went to church with the family. While I was in church a friend of the family, Steve, who ran the local 4H and was a judge in the competition, would pick up Crocket and take him to the fairgrounds. He would always tie him to a fence at the entry gate and leave my stuff alongside. The people at the gate knew that I would be there by 12:30 and watched him until I arrived. That's what people did for each other those days in small towns.

After church I would go home and change and my parents would drive me into town, where Crocket was always happy to see me. My parents rarely stayed to watch. At the end of the day, Steve would take me back to the barn where I had to clean my equipment, clean the stall, and feed my horse. After I tucked him in for the night, I made the mile walk home ready for some food and a good night's sleep.

I learned that Midge went on to study equine management at the University of Louisville in Kentucky and rode on a regular basis her entire life. In 1978 she became a PATH Certified instructor and became proficient in teaching all the various training programs such as Therapeutic Riding, Horses for Heroes, Yoga on Horseback, Silver Saddles for seniors, and Barn Rats for children. Midge told me that over the years she's seen and done just about everything and continues to enjoy teaching as if it was still her first lesson.

Midge is worried that her age and health are catching up with her and this probably will be her last year as an instructor.

DEBBIE – NEW INSTRUCTOR

In my early exposure to Debbie, she was the exact stereotype of my vision of today's horsewoman. She came from a well to do family and was exposed to riding as a young girl with private lessons and her own horse at the age of ten. I learned of her travels to horse competitions, both in and out of state with all the trappings. The way she described it, all her social and daily life revolved around dressage riding and competitions; with weekly lessons and weekend travel many weekends throughout the year. Money was not an issue, as her parents fully supported her passion.

After college she married a successful entrepreneur, and continued riding, while raising a family. Then at age fifty, she found herself an "empty nester" but still wanted an active life. Her husband's company is in full growth mode and her dual career of mother and rider is now down to just riding.

As she tells it, "Todd was content, but I needed something more. I had been aware of the Flatlanders Program through the riding community, and it intrigued me. As I learned more about the program, I saw an opportunity for me to expand my passion and become an instructor in the program."

Becoming PATH certified consists of having to complete a one-year course of 1) an extensive workshop on PATH standards, 2) twenty-five hours of teaching riding lessons while being monitored by a mentor, 3) an on-site instructor riding test, and 4) teaching a PATH approved riding lesson to two program riders. Given her past riding experience she did not anticipate any problems with becoming an instructor although reality quickly set in.

"I failed my first attempt and quickly had to swallow a 'humble pill' before I could move forward. Teaching challenged riders was eye opening to me, never having been exposed to physical, developmental, and emotional handicaps and the unique needs they present to learning. As I approached this portion of the certification the second time around, I got a much deeper understanding of the lives of the riders and their families and how it differed so much from my experience. Once completed however, I learned about the profound impact the program could make in their lives and the critical importance of my role as instructor, in making it happen."

Phase 2 also presented its surprises, requiring passing a personal riding test and 25 hours of teaching practice lessons while being monitored by a mentor, who in Debbie's case was Midge, Flatlanders senior instructor, with whom she had formed a bit of a mother/daughter relationship.

Preparing for the riding test was far different than she expected. Instead of merely demonstrating the ability to ride and control the horse, instructor candidates need to demonstrate various commands considering the limitations of the riders they would be teaching.

Debbie would explain to me as she progressed, "PATH requires the what, how, and why to everything. How would I teach a rider how to maintain focus in riding around the ring? How would I teach someone to turn or stop their horse if they had limited control of their hands or arms? How would I protect the horse from kicks and weight shifting from a rider who has difficulty controlling their body movements? How do you communicate instructions to a rider with developmental limitations? This portion of the program opened a whole new challenge for me in an area that I formerly thought I was an expert, which intrigued me and required my full commitment to this role."

It had been almost a year and Debbie was on the cusp of her certification. The final requirement was being judged in teaching a lesson. She must travel to a testing site, get introduced to both a new horse and client case, and the following day demonstrate a lesson plan which she developed for that specific rider. Midge was able to accompany her but could not participate in any of the lesson planning or execution.

Here's Debbie's account of her experience getting certified:

I was constantly asking Midge whether or not I was ready. The first portions of the certification had certainty taught me how different handicapped riding is from my past experience and I wasn't sure I could remember everything as I understand that they could be a bit nitpicky in their evaluations. The night before, I had made a list of all the things that I had to think about, and this was AFTER I put together my lesson plan:

> Horse selection - making sure the horse has the right movement for the rider, making sure horse is not too wide or narrow

Check the girth before mounting and twice again during the lesson. Also need to check it before going into trot or canter

Make sure the gate is closed

Check position and balance of rider

Keep rider in your sight AT ALL TIMES, no rider should be behind you

Riders must keep safe distance from each other

Never step backwards

With every instruction, you must explain WHAT you're asking, HOW the rider will do what you're asking, and WHY.

Don't just say "Good job." Say instead "Good job looking to the left, good job staying in 2 point etc."

I just didn't know if I could remember it all!

In the back of my head however I kept hearing Midge's voice saying, "Don't worry Debbie, I have seen you over these last weeks of lessons and you have done it all. Just relax, you'll do fine."

The next day at the test, my riders were 20 minutes late which didn't help with the nerves. But once they got there and I got started, things fell into place. All the hard work and support of my mentors paid off. And......I passed!!

One of my favorite riders is Clint who is 27-years-old and has advanced cerebral palsy since birth. He has very limited control of his movements, rigid limbs, unsteady walking even with help and an inability to speak; yet he is the most loveable person you would ever meet. From an outside perspective it may seem that his lessons are essentially just a horse ride, yet his father says the benefits are beyond what can be measured, and he can clearly see it in Clint's behavior.

It takes two volunteers to help mount him on the horse, and despite his condition, he has amazing balance in the saddle. Our lesson consists of the usual walk on, whoa, and right and left turns with the side walkers pulling on the reins. Occasionally Clint will quickly raise and lower the reins a few times and voice a sound to show us he is in control and having fun. Sometimes I will ask him to say, "walk on" and he will just stare at me and show that smile.

I asked Clint's father one day what he thought it might feel like to have cerebral palsy. He said that it is essentially having some muscles that don't work properly. Some are weak, and some are too tight, and they occasionally have spasticity flare ups. It is very hard to execute certain movements and Clint tires quickly. He went on to say that cerebral palsy is brain damage that Clint was born with and that it's not a disease. Physical therapy helps but unfortunately cannot magically make his legs straighten out on their own when stretching.

Clint's father was very thankful for all the encouragement and support that he has gotten and feels that Clint's quality of life has greatly improved. More importantly it was the first time he just got to be 'Clint' and not the child with several disabilities. It may be hard to know exactly how Clint feels about his riding experience, but the spark in his eyes and his devilish smile conveys so much.

Mary – Experienced Instructor

It is amazing to me how the different paths of the instructors all seemed to converge at Flatlanders. Mary has been working her entire life at Flatlanders since she was a teenager, and it was called Cooper's Ranch. She came from a middle-class family and never had the opportunity to be exposed to horses until she was in the eleventh grade. At age 17, thirty years before Rachel took ownership of the Flatlanders Ranch, the old Cooper's Ranch was looking for workers to help maintain the six horses they boarded, and she tells of becoming one of their barn workers. Five days a week she would arrive a 6 am to feed and put out the horses, then she'd return after school to clean out their stalls and fed them again. She remembers that some of her friends would kid her, calling her 'pooper scooper', but the money helped her family and generated a little spending money for her.

Over the years the owners treated her more like a daughter and taught her how to ride. After graduating high school, she started working in an insurance agency but rode as often as she could. Her riding continued to improve and soon she was helping the Coopers to teach riding lessons, becoming an instructor herself a few years later. After marrying, she soon went to part-time work at the insurance agency so that she could teach full-time

Ten years ago, after the change of ownership to Flatlanders Ranch, she continued on with Rachel, as one of the Flatlanders first certified instructors. Overall, she has been

83

teaching now for 35 years and especially enjoys working with special needs riders.

When speaking about her life as an instructor Mary says, "When I started my training as a PATH instructor, they told us that we'd be working to teach life skills. But what they don't tell us is while you're teaching someone, they'll also be teaching you. My experience here has been a perfect fit to the rest of my life."

One day when we were between lessons, I asked Mary if she had any riders that were special to her. As I reflected later on her response, I saw a deeper relationship than I expected and an impact far exceeding my initial observations.

As Mary recounts, "My experience with Down Syndrome riders has shown them to be the most honest, and to have a positive and happy outlook on life. They generally know and accept their limitations yet have the confidence to overcome them and live like everyone else."

"They have taught me it's OK to forgive myself when I have a bad day. There's always tomorrow and a mess-up here and there doesn't mean it's the end of the world. They have taught me to slow down, to ponder, to take the time to just look around and take in this beautiful world and all of the simple joys we are blessed to encounter every day."

"But don't let that laid back attitude be confused with a strong will and independence and my work with Michael confirms that every lesson. When he arrives, he confidently joins his volunteer in grooming and saddling Buddie, often saying, 'I got this.' Saying little, he mounts and says, 'walk on,' often before I'm ready to proceed."

"His father says that he's just like that at home but uses the word stubborn when describing his independence. We've often talked about what happens when Michael is grown, and his parents can no longer take care of him. Fortunately, Michael is independent enough to live on his own with support. He even sees himself married someday. What many people don't realize is although his IQ is lower than average, he has the same emotions and desires that we all have."

"In the arena he is one of my best riders, responding to all of my instructions and quickly advancing to trotting and now cantering. I've suggested he enter the state competition this summer and I think he will do well."

Mary's learning experience from Michael is something that we have all enjoyed. There are times that the student becomes the teacher especially in their perspective on living. Acceptance and appreciation of the life they have and their openness and honesty in interacting with others serves as an example to all of us. These riders give us the opportunity to learn something every lesson and we become better people for it.

CHAPTER 5

VOLUNTEER SERVICE – GIVING BACK

The world is changing and one of the values that is changing along with it is the concept of service and giving back to the community. The concept of formal volunteer service has evolved over the last fifty years, but the tradition of helping each other is longstanding. I've been involved in many not-for-profit organizations in my career, and it seems that people, especially those later in life, are becoming increasingly reluctant to getting involved in volunteer work anymore. My friends know me for my very active life, juggling my time between different organizations which take up much of my 'spare' time, yet a lot of them can't seem to understand why I do it all for free.

During my six years at Flatlanders, I have enjoyed my weekly visits and the many memories that the experience has given me. Yet often times when I bring up my time here to my friends, I'm met with silence, or a perplexed look and the conversation quickly moves on to other topics. Today's attachment to social media seems to take priority over interest and involvement in service to the community. We are all focused on our own personal goals so "I just don't have the time to get involved" is a phrase I constantly hear, especially from my retired friends. The saying is, "If you need something done, ask a busy person."

I think this attitude is not so much that no one wants to help, but rather it is merely a matter of making helping a priority. Financial donations are critical but personal service is even more valuable. To encourage more service we need to better communicate the value of the experience to the individual. Organizations, in general, emphasize the value of the volunteers to their purpose rather than demonstrating its value to the volunteers themselves. This seems to be proven so often by retiring volunteers when you hear them say, "I've gotten more back from my work here than I've ever given to it."

As I said earlier, we all take our physical health for granted until that life changing event occurs and everything is turned upside down. To our riders, rehabilitation of the body is hard and sometimes feels impossible, but mental rehabilitation is often more difficult. As a volunteer I got to see first-hand that restoration happen right before my eyes. To encourage people to get involved, we need to not only communicate the community good being performed, but how the volunteers themselves also benefit from being engaged.

It is that personal satisfaction hook that seems to be a key driver to soliciting volunteer involvement; the lack of general understanding of what the program is all about and how it impacts not only our riders, but also the volunteers who serve.

The following experiences of the Flatlanders' volunteers that I witnessed, will hopefully help provide that connection in order to continue and expand the much needed volunteer support of therapeutic riding.

TED – NEWBIE VOLUNTEER

Over the last few years, I have become quite disillusioned about society's concept of service. I was especially concerned about our youth and how that selflessness and concern for others might become part of their lives. Over the years we have had some troubled youth assigned to our program as part of a community service agreement, but true volunteering seems to take a back seat to a myriad of sports and other extracurricular activities. While we seem to have some young girls engaged primarily because of their interest in riding, young males are rare. This continues throughout all age groups, with men representing 20- 30% of our instructors and volunteers.

So, I was surprised and happy to see 15-year-old Ted arrive for volunteer training. Ted just finished the first semester of his freshman year in high school and made the Honor Club. At his first meeting he learned that the Club was active in community service, encouraging its members to reach out and help in our area. They were especially involved with low-income families, providing after school activities in conjunction with county special services. His family has always been active in their church and his older sister and brother were involved with the Big Brother/Sister program.

As with most of his peers he was interested in working with the Honor Club but was already active in sports and had a scheduling problem in getting involved. His mother's friend was a volunteer at Flatlanders and suggested that he might be interested in working there as part of the Saturday morning Program. So, one day he drove over with his mother to see what it was all about.

As I took him around, I learned that he knew nothing about horses, but was taught by his parents about the responsibility to give back. After about 20 minutes he said to me, "Quite honestly, I'm very excited after being told that one of my first responsibilities is called mucking (cleaning poop out of the horse's stalls). And then after that I get to fill water buckets and sweep the barn floor; not exactly my idea of community service."

I then took him out to the arena where he saw a therapy riding lesson with Clint, a boy with cerebral palsy, and his attitude quickly changed. after a few minutes he said, "Up to now I've had minimal contact with a handicapped person, and now here was someone, my own age, riding a horse despite major control issues of his body. There was someone leading the horse for him and walkers on each side to help if needed. I then learned that my involvement in the volunteer program would also include assisting riders as a leader and/or side walker. That did it for me and I signed on that day."

As with all group activities, there is always some rookie initiation, which welcomes and binds the new person into the group. It is no different at Flatlanders, and Ted's welcome happened during his first week as a volunteer. As Ted's tells the story, "It was an especially hot day, 93 degrees with high humidity. I was told that we might not even have lessons because of the heat, so the instructors limited their lessons to trail rides through the woods, keeping the horses in the shade most of the time. When Buddie finished his lesson, I took off his saddle, he was totally soaked with sweat and Mary suggested that I give him a bath to help cool him down."

"As I sprayed him with the hose, I could sense that he was experiencing the same 'Ahhhhh, don't stop' feeling that I have in the shower after crew practice in the heat. I hosed him down for about 10 minutes and I wasn't sure what to do next as he stood dripping."

"Mary then gave me what's called a sweat scraper to trowel off the water and then told me to give him a good brushing, extending his spa treatment to about a half hour."

"Now looking beautiful, cool, and clean, I proceeded to slowly walk him back to his pasture and let him free to enjoy the rest of the afternoon. As I was walking back to the barn, I saw that everyone was laughing. 'What's so funny?' I asked. They all pointed and when I turned around, I saw clean Buddie rolling in the dirt. All my work now in a cloud of dust, with mud all over him!"

"Mary came over with a big smile on her face. 'It has happened to all of us,' she said. 'Horses roll in the dirt to help keep the flies away. All Buddie was doing was putting that protection screen back on after you washed him. We normally leave them out until their fully dried off, so it's only dust, not mud."

"Welcome to the life of a Newbie."

Volunteers normally have a set schedule as to days, instructors, and riders. Ted's time is Saturday mornings working with Mary and now after two months they have become a good team. But the program needs to be flexible, and one Saturday Mary was going on vacation to see her kids in Pennsylvania, so Ted was now working with Margaret and a different rider and horse. Although catching, grooming, and saddling were the same tasks, doing them for a different horse, in this case Garfield, is a very different experience.

Most days Garfield is no different than Willie, his friend from Ohio, but on that particular day he didn't want to work and sensing Ted was a newbie, kept walking away from him refusing to put on his halter. After about ten minutes of chasing him, Debbie came out and showed Ted how to put a rope around his neck making it easier to control him and put his halter on. Once Garfield saw her, he knew that his little ruse was over.

No two riders, instructors, or horses are the same and it was a lesson learned for Ted. "Up until then all my rider interaction had been with Michael, a very social, independent rider with Down Syndrome. He would let me know what he needed, which he clearly did, otherwise don't get in the way. Now in almost in a complete role reversal, I was working with an autistic rider, whose lessons were structured to keep their attention and focus during their swings from brilliant to total disconnection."

"Debbie too, was a very different instructor, she did the same things, stretching, turning, in and out of the cones and trotting, just in a more methodological and deliberate manner. Between horse, rider, and instructor, it felt like my first day as a volunteer all over again and I was starting to get a sense of how flexible and varied equine therapy is, among horse rider and instructor."

SALLY – SPIRITUAL VOLUNTEER

Sally takes a road less traveled in her work at Flatlanders. In her mind, therapeutic riding is a simple straight line of energy from the horse to the rider, to the instructor, to the volunteer. Her path to Flatlanders is unique, beginning at the racetrack.

As a teenager during summers in college, before getting her teaching degree, she worked at Nottingham Downs, a small racecourse in New York, hot walking horses; walking and cooling them down after workouts and races. While she didn't realize it at the time, horses have a natural calm and energy which can take over those in their presence. You certainly couldn't see that when they were on the track, but it was obvious in the early morning and late afternoons in the barn, when it was just the two of them, where she often found herself unconsciously starting a two-way conversation with the horses.

She then was an elementary school art and physical education teacher for twenty years, 10 years ago incorporating yoga into physical education as a pilot program, which has since expanded into mediation and mindfulness and now is being replicated in other schools throughout the state. She proudly says that "Parents don't realize the pressures placed on our preteens today, especially through social media, and this program has shown to help in relieving that stress."

Moving to Vermont 10 years ago after a late marriage, she continued on as an art teacher in high school. "As an art teacher in Vermont, I often take my class into nature as a way to motivate them in expressing their feelings about what they see, rather than just working from pictures and books. On a friend's recommendation, one of these trips was to the Flatlanders Ranch to observe and draw horses grazing in their pasture. That trip was an unbelievable success for both the class and myself. As the class worked on their assignment, I was taken by the tranquility and peace I was experiencing, which rivaled what I felt in meditation."

After researching it more, Sally learned that Flatlanders offered a yoga on horseback program which she soon joined, finding the experience unique, and the energy invigorating. Since that time, Sally now also participates in our volunteer program seeing much of that same energy being experienced by the handicapped riders.

Sensing energy throughout nature, Sally made another connection in the program, overlooked by many. Most barns always have a cat as a constant visitor. No one seems to know where they came from or even where they go at night, but it's always around, doing the job of keeping the barn free of rodents, keeping the horses company and always available for the stroke of a visitor.

Although The Flatlanders Program revolves around horses and riders, the barn cat is also an integral part of the program. Virtually no rider begins their lesson without first visiting with our cat, Cowboy, a black and white basic feline. Greetings of "Hello, how pretty you look today," paired with the inevitable stroking provides calm and is the perfect transition into a ride. Cowboy also provides a friendly companion to siblings and parents alike during lessons.

To Sally the energy connection with Cowboy is no different from the horses, as she saw one quiet afternoon last summer, when the silence was broken by the screams of little Mary. Sally remembers clearly, "It sounded like the four-year-old was being dragged to her execution but in reality it was just a meltdown from a change in medication. Meltdowns are part of daily life here but as a volunteer only seeing it on an occasional basis, it can generate a pain in the pit of your stomach that you can't do anything about. How parents deal with this on a regular basis is beyond me."

Just as her mother carried her in, Cowboy came to the rescue, by his mere presence. Mary, upon seeing him, quickly stopped crying, and started saying his name, the tears still streaming down her cheeks. Only sobbing a little now, Mary was lowered to the ground where she immediately started petting the cat. The change was almost immediate.

From my readings I knew about the impact animals in general can have on humans, but now I was seeing it profoundly happening right before my eyes. After about five minutes I said, "Mary are you ready to ride Chongos?" and her lesson began.

Throughout her career Sally has studied energy, meditation, and horses, and soon started to practice Reiki, a Japanese technique for stress reduction and relaxation that also promotes healing. It is administered by 'laying on hands' and is based on the idea that an unseen life force energy flows through us and is what causes us to be alive. Given their natural energy, horses practice a form of Reiki on those around them and, as Sally came to find out, is a major component of equine therapy success.

Margaret – Retired Volunteer

Margaret has one of the most unique and varied backgrounds of all our volunteers, coming from a career in international business. She and her husband have traveled all around the world, experiencing different cultures and lifestyles, living both in Europe and the far east. She has no children, nor had she experienced a traditional home base until three years ago when they both retired and decided to live in Vermont.

Although my background was far different than Margaret, I was curious how she was adjusting to retirement. Strangely, after listening to her for a while, I felt like I was looking in a mirror. During one of our first lessons working together Margaret shared her story with me.

"In the beginning, retirement wasn't easy after such a busy career. I clearly was not prepared for the immediate lack of structure and challenge and began searching for a new purpose and meaning. In the first months I did the usual new retirement activities; taking classes at the local college, joining a book club, and doing on-line assessments to help identify the next chapter of my life. It all helped, but there was still something missing. After six months of searching, my friend Sally introduced me to Flatlanders at a beef and beer fundraiser and suggested that I might want to try volunteering with her."

"I had never ridden in my life nor had any real contact with horses, but the program quickly drew me. One of the first experiences I had was with a rider named Cate."

After bringing Garfield in from the pasture, taking off his fly sheet, grooming and fly spraying him, we were ready for Cate, one of my favorite riders. Cate is the cutest five-year-old autistic child, with a quiet but happy and friendly personality. She drifts off at times into her own little world with thoughts that we will never know, returning a few minutes later back to our world again.

On this day we were going on the Sensory Trail where it would be cooler than in the arena. This gave me the opportunity to interact more with Cate than her usual lesson.

Our first stop was the tick-tack-toe board - Cate vs. me. I bragged that I have never lost a match and Cate just smiled and turned the block to the first X in the center. I turned the top left block to O and Cate the top left block to X. I said, "Now I 've got you," as I turned the middle left block to O. Cate looked at the board as she got ready to turn over the middle right block, when I said, "I'm going to win." She then moved her hand to the bottom left and turned over the X as she said, "No, I win!" Showing complete surprise I said, "Oh no! I never lose, but you beat me today. My perfect record gone," And with that we moved on with a smile on everyone's face.

After going over the bridge we went over to the kids' favorite stop, the 'Car Wash.' It is a series of foam noodles which are hung horizontally between two trees and also hang down from above. The horse stops in the middle and the kids are brushed by the noodles from all directions always eliciting squeals and giggles.

Next was the see saw where the horse climbs up one side and down the other as the board rocks down. Cate looked a bit worried, but I held her leg and told her to relax. As the board struck the ground on the other side, there was a quick look of panic on her face which changed to a smile when I said, "You did it, you did it, great job!"

We then went on to the tree with a tire hanging down from a limb, for the football toss. The horse stopped and Cate took the small ball to throw through the tire. This is hard for both horse and rider because throws often hit the horse in the head or bounce back against their bodies off the tire. With a look of determination and focus, Cate did well getting the ball through three out of five times.

The last and most challenging stop for the horse is the musical chimes hanging between two trees. The horse has to deal with three issues, often simultaneously. The rider making a loud noise hitting the chimes with a metal stick, which then often continues down striking the horse in the head or shoulder. And if that's not enough, the rider is constantly shifting their weight to play the music. Fortunately for Garfield, Cate's musical rendition was relatively uneventful.

For many of our autistic rider's music is an important component of our program and for some reason country and western songs seem to be a favorite. I'm not sure why, maybe it's the calm story telling nature of the music.

Normally this was the end of the Sensory Trail ride, but on that day, Cate made it memorable for all of us. After playing her music, Cate just stared out towards the driveway. Midge gestured for us to all just stay still as we stood there no knowing where Cate had gone with her thoughts. After about 30 seconds a car started to drive down the driveway and Cate said, "Ford

Taurus" and we all looked at each other in surprise. A second car was following, and Cate promptly said "Chevy Malibu." Moving on, now in total disbelief of what we just experienced, we left the Sensory Trail.

When we got back to the barn, we immediately shared our experience with Cate's mother, Ellen who said, "Oh, I guess I never told you, but Cate loves cars and trucks and can name just about any vehicle she sees. It started about a year ago and she will just ask the name when she sees it or hears about it on TV, then it's engrained in her memory."

Amazing. It went even further after I showed her my car, because from then on, whenever I would ask her what kind of car I drove, she would say, "Lexus, and Mommy drives a Toyota." I'll never forget that day!

Margaret has also started riding in the Silver Saddles program. She now says that after two years at Flatlanders, these two activities not only fill her day, but more importantly have given her the start of the next chapter of her life. She shared that she has now settled into a new, relaxed lifestyle with service replacing much of the work portion of her last chapter. In addition to Flatlanders, she also has become involved with her local church and its senior Meals on Wheels program.

It quickly became clear that for both Margaret and I service is its own reward, far different then money, stature, or power, and provides a deep sense of satisfaction in helping others.

Cowboy Ed – Western Volunteer

In the eastern part of the states, riding is a sport dominated by women beginning at a young age. In the west, it is just the opposite, where it is a way of life for young males, not just a sport. Ed grew up on a 500-acre ranch with 1,500 head of cattle. He learned all about horses as partners in everyday work life. The only sport side of riding in the west are rodeos, where horse and rider got to compete and demonstrate their skills as a one. Ed's skill was cattle roping. He wasn't your typical cowboy in appearance, standing only 5 feet 6 inches and weighing only 145 pounds, but he still won his fair share of events.

As with many families at that time, Ed and his brothers wanted to get away from the hard and often financially risky business of ranching and chart their own lives. But in 1968 the Vietnam war was going strong, and the draft was in place. As Ed remembers, "At the age of 18 everyone had to register for the draft and I was unfortunate to draw number 68, which virtually guaranteed that I was going into the service that year. My options were two years in the Army or Marines or four years in the Navy or Air Force. Not fully embracing the Marine philosophy, I choose the Army and like clockwork, in 6 months I was in Vietnam. I have kept those experiences to myself and was more fortunate than some of my friends, having returned reasonably intact."

After his time in Vietnam, and with the help of the GI Bill, Ed was able to attend college and pursue a career in electronics. Over the years he traveled around the country, raised a family, and is now retired in Vermont. During all that time however, he made sure that horses were always part of his life, both as an owner and rider. He and his horse Toby have been together now for almost twenty years and the bond they have is as strong as ever.

Ed knew nothing about therapy riding until he moved to Vermont and boarded Toby at the Flatlanders Ranch. At first, he just enjoyed the wonderful riding trails that Vermont has to offer. Soon he found himself volunteering at the Flatlanders equine program and sharing his riding experience with others.

"I've kept my western appearance; cowboy hat and boots and as such, am known as Cowboy Ed here. I've bulked up a bit to 165 pounds and now sport a reddish mustache. During open houses and sometimes lessons, I like to show off my roping skills as a bit of side entertainment."

Ed clearly remembers the day that he became a volunteer, and Rachel welcomed him into what she calls the transition to the next level of riding - committing oneself to others' riding experience rather than one's own.

Ed says, "When I decided to join the Flatlanders program, the focus of my passion changed from my personal and practical relationship with a horse to helping others, especially veterans with special needs, to develop their own equine bonding and skills. Soon I was getting more personal joy and satisfaction from the experience of others than I did from my own riding."

Since he became a volunteer, Ed has focused his time on the Horses for Heroes program, saying, "Like most veterans from my time, I don't speak about Nam. People just won't understand. But my time with Ken and Warren has given me the opportunity to express of a lot of those feelings with others who can relate. I will tell everyone that in the three years that I have been involved, I feel that I have gotten more from this program that I have given."

Like Ed, the stories I tell everyone lately are about my riders at The Flatlanders Ranch. My life is now in two worlds. Although somewhat opposites, they each bring me great joy and satisfaction. While enjoying my family, golf, and travel, I look forward to my regular lessons with our riders.

I think there are a lot of people like me, who later in life are drawn into therapeutic programs as a way of giving back. We don't do it for money or prestige, we just do it because we love it.

CHAPTER 6

EPILOGUE

Horses and Humans

by Gene Arnone

There once was a rider, an instructor, a volunteer, and a horse, who went on the internet every day, looking for help in finding their way. They had often heard of Equine Assisted Riding and Activities (EAAT), but they had never participated in it; so how could they know what it was?

It so happened one morning that the Flatlanders Ranch started an EAAT program, right in the town where they lived. Of course, they could not know what it was just by reading, so they thought that by participating they could learn what it was all about.

The rider was the first one to have a lesson. "Well, well!" he said, "Now I know all about EAAT, it is a way for me to help overcome my challenges."

The next was an instructor who became PATH certified. "My brother," he said, "You are mistaken. It defines my purpose in life, a clear path for me to follow."

The volunteer who signed up to help said, "Both of you are wrong. Anybody who knows anything, can see that this is a chance for community service to make a difference."

The horse stomped his front hoof and nudged the other three. "Oh, how blind you are!" he said. "It is very plain to me, that this is a chance for horse and man to bond as nature intended."

When the season was over and the snow began to fall, the program closed for the winter and the four of them told their friends about EAAT, each believing that they knew just what the program was all about; and each calling the others ignorant, because they did not agree with him.

Equine Assisted Riding is many things to many people and hopefully this story helped us to see the elephant of how Horses + Humans = Positive Changes.

Our Hoof Beats Are Many, But Our Hearts Beat As One.